Timeline of monuments

Follow the timeline to learn more about India's monuments through some of the key events in history.

Dashavatara Temple at Deogarh, one of the earliest known structural temples, is built under the Gupta kings.

Vasco da Gama, a Portugese explorer, lands in Calicut to open a trade route from Europe to the East.

Babur commissions Kabuli Bagh Mosque to mark his victory a year before, over Ibrahim Lodhi, the last ruler of the Delhi Sultanate.

c.500	1206	1311	1498	1501	1503	1527

Qutb-ud-din Aibak establishes Mamluk (also known as "Slave") dynasty of Delhi, which lay the foundation of the Delhi Sultanate.

Alai Minar, an unfinished ambitious project, is commissioned by Alauddin Khilji, one of the most powerful rulers of the Delhi Sultanate.

Continued at → back of book

Cochin becomes the first European settlement in India after its ruler agrees to be under Portuguese protection.

Golkonda Fort becomes the seat of government of the Qutb Shahi dynasty of Hyderabad's Golkonda Sultanate.

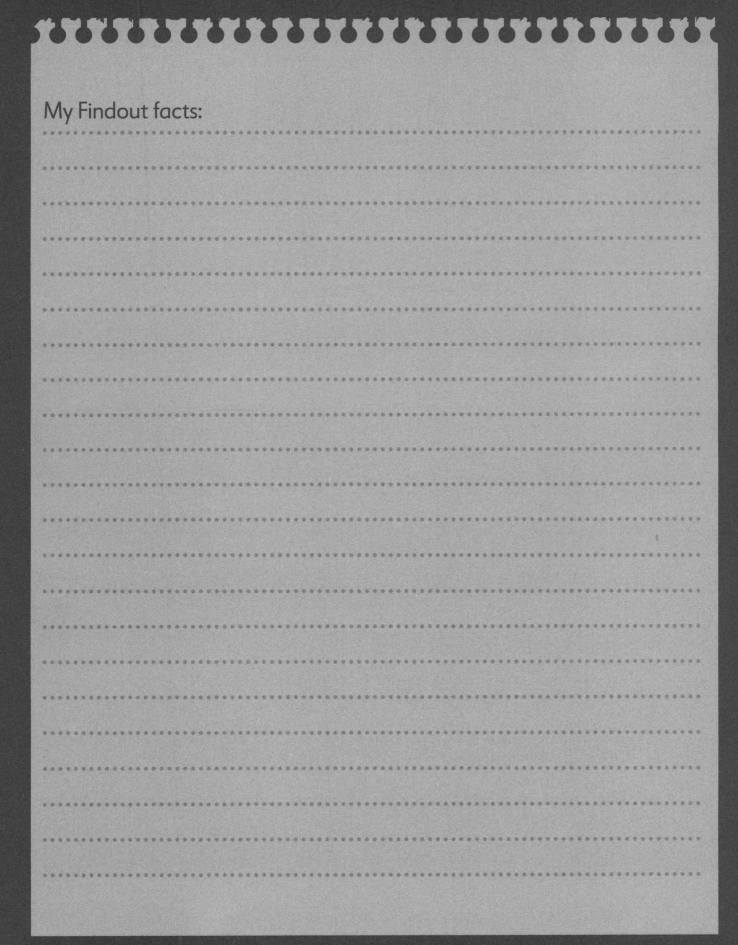

My Findout facts:

DK findout!

Monuments
of India

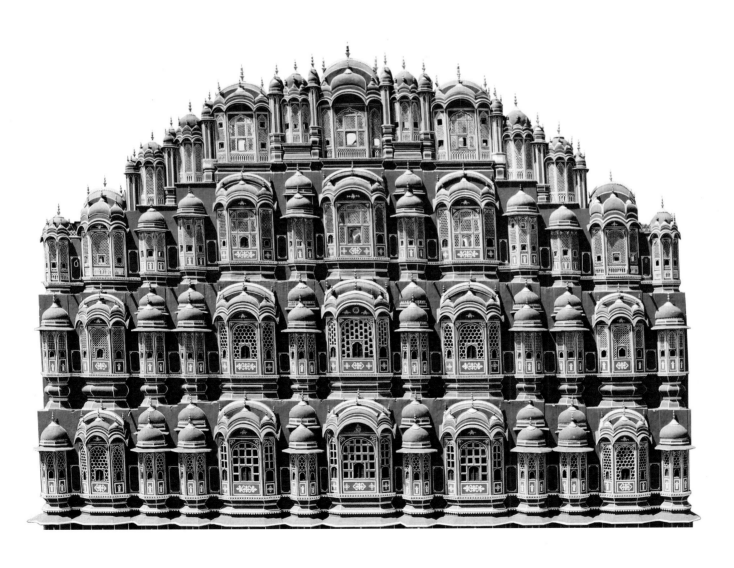

DK | Penguin Random House

Editors Shalini Agrawal, Mark Silas
Designers Nidhi Mehra, Nehal Verma,
Seepiya Sahni
Senior picture researcher Sumedha Chopra
Managing editor Alka Thakur
Managing art editor Romi Chakraborty
Picture research manager Taiyaba Khatoon
Senior DTP designers Neeraj Bhatia
DTP designers Sachin Gupta, Syed Md. Farhan
Pre-production manager Narender Kumar
Senior jacket designer Dheeraj Arora
Managing director Aparna Sharma

First American Edition, 2020
Published in the United States by DK Publishing
1450 Broadway, Suite 801, New York, NY 10018

Copyright © 2020 Dorling Kindersley Limited
DK, a Division of Penguin Random House LLC
20 21 22 23 24 10 9 8 7 6 5 4 3 2 1
001–320486–Oct/2020

A catalog record for this book
is available from the Library of Congress.
ISBN: 978-0-7440-2188-2 (Hardcover)
ISBN: 978-0-7440-2187-5 (Paperback)

DK books are available at special discounts when purchased in
bulk for promotions, premiums, fund-raising, or educational use.
For details, contact: DK Publishing Special Markets,
1450 Broadway, Suite 801, New York, NY 10018
SpecialSales@dk.com

Printed and bound in China

For the curious
www.dk.com

Contents

Motif from Gwalior Fort

Golden lotus,
Meenakshi Temple

Pashupati seal

The Buddha

THIS BRONZE PANEL ORIGINALLY EXECUTED BY SIR GOSCOMBE JOHN R. A. FOR THE PEDESTAL OF THE STATUE OF THE LATE EARL OF MINTO VICEROY & GOVERNOR-GENERAL OF INDIA 1905-1910. WAS PRESENTED TO THE TRUSTEES OF THE VICTORIA MEMORIAL HALL BY THE DOWAGER COUNTESS OF MINTO.

Bronze panel showing the
Viceroy's royal procession

3

What is a monument?

A monument is a building, structure, or statue built to honor a significant person or event. Any unique piece of architecture can be called a monument, too. Something built in the past can be called a monument if it tells us about our heritage.

Archaeological remains
The ruins of a city built by our ancestors can help us piece together the past. The remains at Hampi tell the temple city's history as the seat of the Vijayanagara empire from the 14th to 16th century.

Virupaksha Temple

Types of monuments

India is known for its monuments that were built during different periods. While many have disappeared over time, others have survived and give a sense of history.

Kumbhalgarh Fort, Rajasthan

Historical buildings

Historically significant forts and palaces, religious shrines, or public buildings can be called monuments. A building noted for its unique architecture can also be called a monument.

India Gate, Delhi

Gateways and arches

Triumphal arches and gateways meant to celebrate an event were built throughout history. Besides recording the event for future generations, each gateway reflects the architectural style of its era.

Gyarah Murti, Delhi

Memorial statues

Commissioned by kings and other rulers, and later, by the government, memorial statues pay tribute to key figures, keeping them alive in public memory.

Early monuments

Early humans lived in caves, hunted wild animals, and gathered plants for food. As they started to settle, they built towns and cities, and created civilizations. The drawings left behind on the walls of caves and the ruins of their cities help us understand how early humans lived.

The Bhimbetka Rock Shelter

More than 1,000 rock shelters, found in Bhopal, Madhya Pradesh, are among the oldest monuments in the world. About 500 caves are covered in paintings, most of which date from 8000 to 5000 BCE.

Prehistoric

Line paintings of animals, such as bear and bison, as well as human figures hunting with spears and bows, can be seen in the caves at Bhimbetka. It was common to use red pigment for animals and green for humans.

Historic
These relatively newer drawings are more elaborate and have many details. Animals, such as deer and elephants, appear in these paintings.

Lothal

A major settlement in the Indus Valley, Lothal in Gujarat, had a system of wells for drinking water, and drains to flush away dirty water.

Indus Valley

The Indus Valley civilization lasted from around 3300 to 1300 BCE. Around 2600 BCE, the people began to build the world's first planned cities. Two major cities, Mohenjo-daro and Harappa (both now in Pakistan), are important archaeological sites. They show an advanced city planning and complex drainage system.

The people of the Indus Valley discovered how to make durable bricks using red clay and stones. These have lasted more than 4,000 years.

Harappa

Just as other Indus cities, Harappa was laid out in a grid pattern of streets. The city was packed with mud-brick houses that had multiple stories. Many clay figures, toys, and seals found here tell us how the Indus Valley people lived.

Merchants might have carried small seals to mark goods and sign documents.

Several small terracotta figurines have been unearthed at Harappa.

Petroglyphs

Edakkal caves

Another large rock shelter lies in Edakkal, Kerala. The walls are decorated with carvings called petroglyphs that are believed to date back to 6000 BCE. Some believe that the caves later became the refuge of Jain monks.

Megaliths

Megaliths are monuments made of large slabs of stone. The earliest megaliths in India were created around 1500 BCE. These were largely used in burying the dead. Archaeologists believe that they also served a ceremonial purpose.

Mawphlang
Megalithic graves of the ancestors of the local Khasi people can be found in the sacred forest of Mawphlang, in Meghalaya. Compared to the megaliths of southern India, these are believed to be more recent—only 700 years old.

Dolmens
Shaped like a mushroom, a dolmen is created with four standing slabs of stone, topped by a flat stone. Dolmens that are partly underground might contain personal items, such as pottery, tools, and jewelry, in addition to human remains.

Megalithic graves

Megaliths can be found all over India, although a majority of them are located in the far south and Maharashtra. Mostly burial sites, these sometimes contained items for the dead to use in the afterlife. The practice of making megaliths continues among the Khasis of the Northeast and the Mundas of Jharkhand.

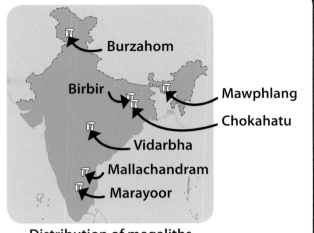

Distribution of megaliths

Burzahom
Birbir
Mawphlang
Chokahatu
Vidarbha
Mallachandram
Marayoor

Menhirs
Menhirs are tall, human-made stones standing upright. They exist either as monoliths ("single stones"), or as part of a group of similar stones. The menhirs at Burzahom, in Kashmir, stand as single stones.

Capstone
A flat slab of stone, the capstone gives the dolmen its table-like appearance. Sometimes, small pieces of stone are placed underneath to level the dolmen properly.

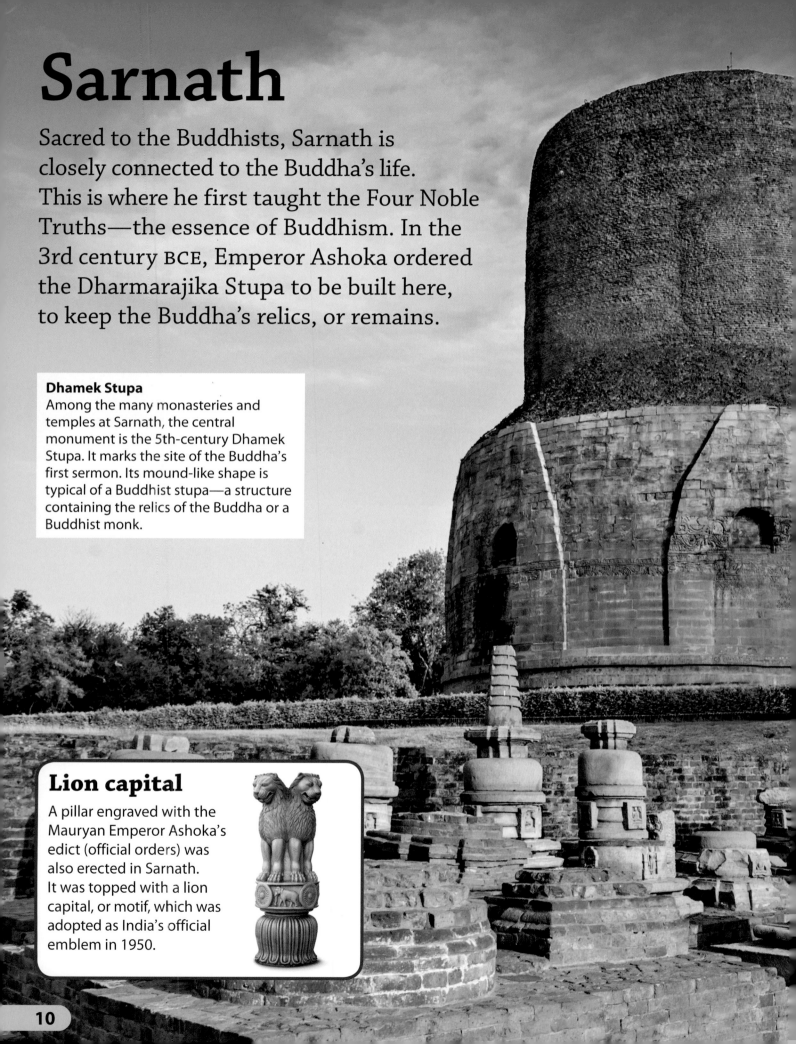

Sarnath

Sacred to the Buddhists, Sarnath is closely connected to the Buddha's life. This is where he first taught the Four Noble Truths—the essence of Buddhism. In the 3rd century BCE, Emperor Ashoka ordered the Dharmarajika Stupa to be built here, to keep the Buddha's relics, or remains.

Dhamek Stupa

Among the many monasteries and temples at Sarnath, the central monument is the 5th-century Dhamek Stupa. It marks the site of the Buddha's first sermon. Its mound-like shape is typical of a Buddhist stupa—a structure containing the relics of the Buddha or a Buddhist monk.

Lion capital

A pillar engraved with the Mauryan Emperor Ashoka's edict (official orders) was also erected in Sarnath. It was topped with a lion capital, or motif, which was adopted as India's official emblem in 1950.

The Enlightened One

Born in around 6th century BCE, Prince Siddhartha gave up his kingdom to find a life without suffering. He was renamed the Buddha, or the Enlightened One.

The Buddha
The Buddha's teachings form the basis of Buddhism. At its center are the Four Noble Truths: suffering exists; it has a cause; the cause is desire; following the path of truth can end all suffering.

Mahabodhi Temple
Originally built by Ashoka, this temple complex in Bodh Gaya, Bihar, contains the bodhi tree, under which the Buddha is believed to have attained enlightenment.

First sermon
The Buddha's first sermon, "The Wheel of Law," is depicted in this carved panel from Sanchi.

Sanchi Stupa

For more than 2,000 years, the stone stupa at Sanchi has stood as a timeless example of Buddhist architecture. It is known for its beautifully carved gateways, or *toranas*, which depict scenes from the Buddha's life.

A square-shaped railing encloses the stone spire, called the *yasti*.

Torana, added in the 1st century CE

The Great Stupa
Ashoka ordered the Buddha's remains to be housed in stupas across his empire. A part of them were kept in the Great Stupa, which was at first a small brick structure. Over time, it was renovated in sandstone and the beautiful *toranas* were added.

Spread of Buddhism

Buddhism rose as a major religion in the 3rd century BCE, under the patronage of Ashoka, the Mauryan ruler who made it his state religion. He encouraged his subjects to become Buddhists. Thousands of Buddhist shrines were built across his kingdom. He also sent representatives abroad to spread the faith.

Ashoka the Great
From 268 to 232 BCE, Ashoka ruled a vast empire, which included nearly all of the Indian subcontinent.

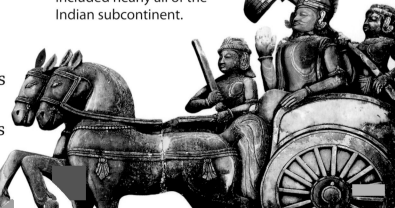

The three tiers of the *yasti* symbolize the three levels of heaven.

Semicircular dome

Jataka tales

The Buddha is believed to have lived 550 lives, or incarnations, before finding enlightenment. The stories of his past lives, called Jataka tales, are carved on the pillars of the *torana*, or the gateways. In one scene, he is shown taming a serpent.

Buddha taming the serpent

The circular pathway allows devotees to walk around the stupa.

Footprints
Early Buddhist monuments suggested the Buddha's presence by showing carved footprints with symbolic images, such as the wheel.

Carved footprints, Sanchi

Maitreya Buddha
Colorful Buddhist icons, including those of Maitreya, or Future Buddha, began to appear as Buddhism spread.

Rock-cut caves

The earliest *chaityas* (prayer halls) and *viharas* (monasteries) were cut into rock faces, in the 2nd century BCE, for Buddhist monks to live and meditate. Other examples of rock-cut caves are the Jain and Hindu temples, which were commissioned by kings and wealthy merchants in the later centuries.

Murals

The walls and ceilings of the Ajanta Caves are decorated with Buddhist murals. The best known of all, Cave 1 famously features the Buddha as Bodhisattva Padmapani (The One with a Lotus in His Hand).

Bodhisattva Padmapani

Ajanta Caves

Featuring *chaityas* and *viharas,* the 30 caves at Ajanta (Maharashtra) are treasured for their murals, created during the 2nd century BCE–5th century CE.

Ellora Caves

The rock-cut cave complex at Ellora (Maharashtra) includes Buddhist monasteries, as well as Jain and Hindu temples, built between 66 and 1000 CE.

Buddhist vihara

Cave 5
The monastery here has a prayer hall featuring a statue of the seated Buddha, with a row of carved pillars on either side.

Indra Sabha Temple

Cave 32
The finest of the Jain temples, Indra Sabha features carved elephants, lions, and Jain *tirthankaras* (past births of Lord Mahavira).

Kailasanath Temple

Cave 16
Dedicated to Lord Shiva, the 8th-century Kailasanath Temple is one of the world's largest rock-cut Hindu shrines.

Temple architecture

India's first temples were modest rock-cut caves. Later, free-standing temples began to be built, giving birth to two distinct styles—Nagara in the north and Dravidian in the south. Large in scale and ornate in design, both styles feature carvings of Hindu deities.

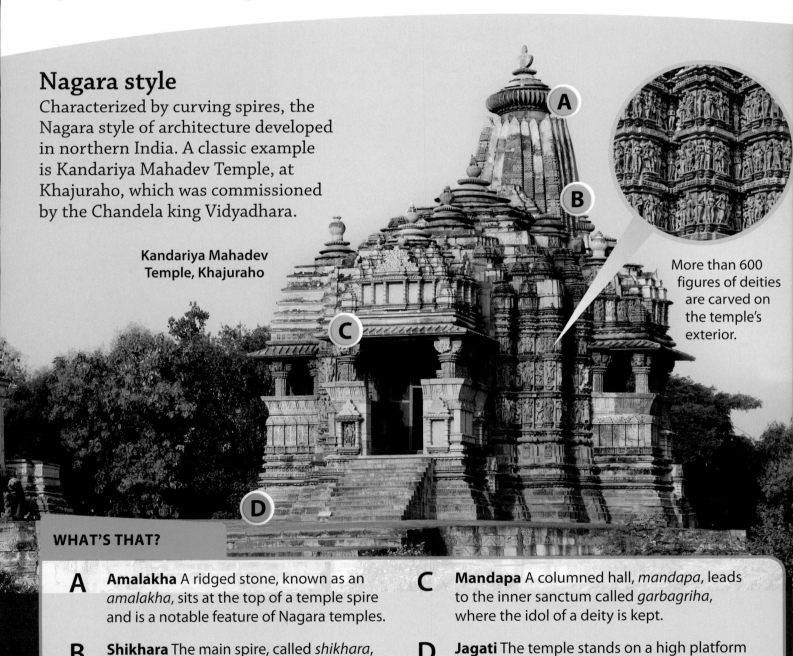

Nagara style

Characterized by curving spires, the Nagara style of architecture developed in northern India. A classic example is Kandariya Mahadev Temple, at Khajuraho, which was commissioned by the Chandela king Vidyadhara.

Kandariya Mahadev Temple, Khajuraho

More than 600 figures of deities are carved on the temple's exterior.

WHAT'S THAT?

A **Amalakha** A ridged stone, known as an *amalakha*, sits at the top of a temple spire and is a notable feature of Nagara temples.

B **Shikhara** The main spire, called *shikhara*, looms over several smaller replicas that surround it.

C **Mandapa** A columned hall, *mandapa*, leads to the inner sanctum called *garbagriha*, where the idol of a deity is kept.

D **Jagati** The temple stands on a high platform made of stone bricks, known as *jagati*. It allows devotees to walk around the temple.

Vesara style

Vesara comes from the Sanskrit word for mule (a hybrid animal). It was developed under the Chalukya kings, and was influenced by both the Nagara and Dravidian styles. Papanatha Temple in the rock-cut complex of Pattadakal was built in the 8th century in the Vesara style.

Nagara-style *shikhara*

Dravidian-style exterior

Papanatha Temple in Pattadakal, Karnataka

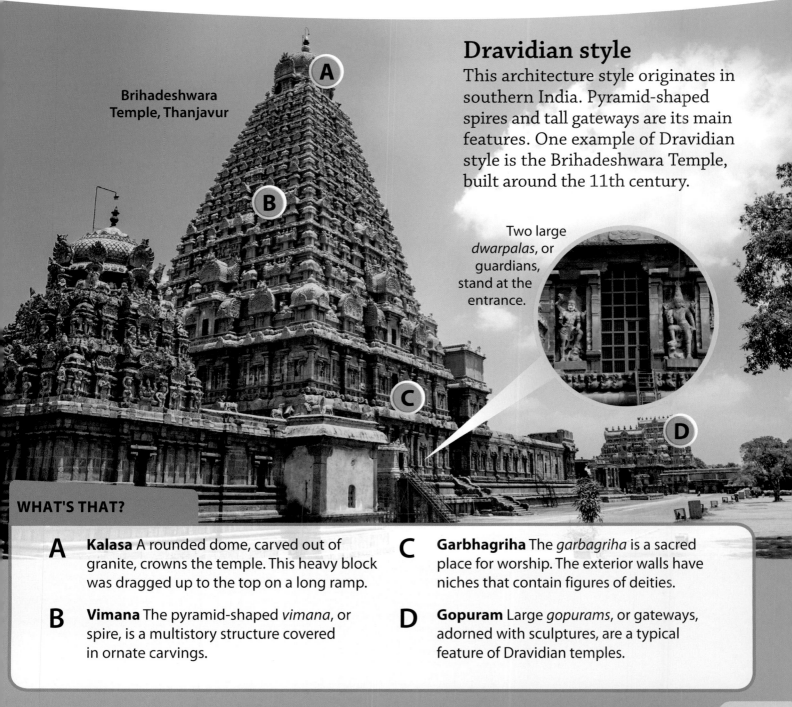

Brihadeshwara Temple, Thanjavur

A

B

C

D

Dravidian style

This architecture style originates in southern India. Pyramid-shaped spires and tall gateways are its main features. One example of Dravidian style is the Brihadeshwara Temple, built around the 11th century.

Two large *dwarpalas*, or guardians, stand at the entrance.

WHAT'S THAT?

A **Kalasa** A rounded dome, carved out of granite, crowns the temple. This heavy block was dragged up to the top on a long ramp.

B **Vimana** The pyramid-shaped *vimana*, or spire, is a multistory structure covered in ornate carvings.

C **Garbhagriha** The *garbagriha* is a sacred place for worship. The exterior walls have niches that contain figures of deities.

D **Gopuram** Large *gopurams*, or gateways, adorned with sculptures, are a typical feature of Dravidian temples.

Temple complexes

India's first free-standing temples were built under the Gupta rule, during the 4th and 5th centuries CE. Later, elaborate temple complexes were commissioned by kings and merchants. Some temples became rich and powerful, expanding into thriving towns. Hampi, once a small village in Karnataka, grew into a temple city and royal capital.

! WOW!

The design of the Shore Temple, in Mamallapuram, allows the first rays of the sun to fall on Lord Shiva.

Mamallapuram

This 7th-century temple complex, in Tamil Nadu, was commissioned by the Pallava king Narasimha Varman I. It features five *rathas* (rock-cut chariots).

Descent of the Ganges

This carving on a massive granite boulder depicts the legend of Ganga's descent from heaven.

Elephant stables

Royal elephants were housed in these stables. There are 11 domes with entries for keepers at the back.

Shore Temple
This 8th-century structural (free-standing) temple features two shrines dedicated to Lord Shiva.

Lakshmana Temple
This shrine of Vishnu is one of the earliest, and best-preserved, temples in the complex.

Khajuraho

This exquisite temple complex, in Madhya Pradesh, was built under the Chandelas between the 10th and 12th centuries. Of the 85 temples thought be built originally, only 25 survive today.

Sculptures
Fine sculptures are carved on the walls of temples, such as the Chitragupta Temple, devoted to the sun.

Vitthala Temple
One of the finest temples in the Hampi complex is devoted to Vitthala, or Vishnu.

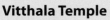

Garuda Shrine, in the form of a chariot, is dedicated to Vishnu's charioteer, Garuda.

Hampi

This temple city was once the capital of the Vijayanagara empire, which was founded in 1336. Built from local granite, temples, statues, forts, and royal complexes still exist here.

Meenakshi Temple

Lying at the heart of the temple town of Madurai, Meenakshi Temple is a striking example of Dravidian architecture. In the 17th century, it served as the chief shrine of the Nayak kings. They added to the existing inner and outer gateways, or *gopurams*, as well as several shrines within the temple complex.

Gopurams
The many inner and outer *gopurams* lead to the shrines built for various gods.

Stucco figures
Shaped like a pyramid, the gateway is decorated with painted sculptures of various deities and animals.

Yali head
Yali, which tops both sides of the roof, is a mythical creature. Though ferocious in appearance, it brings good fortune.

Detail of Shiva
The outer *gopuram* features a carving of the Hindu god Shiva. It shows him holding different weapons in his 16 hands.

Inside the temple

The twin shrines in the complex are dedicated to the Hindu goddess Meenakshi and god Sundaresvara. The halls and corridors are covered in colorful motifs.

Pillared corridor
The corridor surrounds the sacred tank, and leads to Meenakshi's shrine. The ceiling features bright paintings of flowers.

Golden lotus
A sacred tank in the heart of the complex, called Potramarai Kulam, or Golden Lotus Tank, has a gilded flower that appears to be floating in the water.

Konark

Odisha's Konark Temple is one of India's great architectural marvels. Shaped like a giant horse-drawn chariot, it is mounted on carved stone wheels. King Narasimhadeva I of the Eastern Ganga dynasty dedicated it to Surya, the sun god, in 1250. It took 1,200 craftsmen 12 years to build and decorate this temple.

The *rath*, or chariot, of the Sun Temple

Chariot horses

Seven stone horses, which symbolize the seven days of the week, draw the temple-chariot. It carries the sun god on his daily journey across the sky.

Surya
A finely carved statue of the sun god sits against the north wall of the temple. Believed to bring the sun with him, he travels across the skies in his chariot and battles the demons of darkness.

Chariot wheels

The 12 pairs of stone wheels represent the months in a year. The spokes feature finely carved medallions that show scenes from everyday life.

Sculptures

Several sculptures of animals, humans, as well as deities, decorate the temple's roof and walls. These range in size from enormous to small.

A dancer surrounded by mythical beasts

Dancers and mythical beasts
Rows of dancing figures, flanked by terrifying mythical beasts, decorate the walls of the temple.

Hall of Offerings

The dance pavilion, or "Hall of Offerings," was used by musicians and dancers for festivities in honor of Surya.

Riding an elephant, the king receives visitors

Royalty
Foreign leaders would often visit the royal court, bearing gifts. A relief on the temple wall depicts visitors presenting an African giraffe to the king.

Medieval architecture

India's medieval period began with the founding of the Delhi Sultanate by the Mamluk Turks in 1206. It lasted until the end of the Mughal rule in 1707. Under their rule, elements of Indian architecture were borrowed to create an Indianized form of Islamic architecture, known as Indo-Islamic. Two distinct types of the Indo-Islamic style were born—the Imperial and the Mughal.

Qutub Minar, Delhi

Gateways

Huge ceremonial *darwazas* (gateways) were built to symbolize grandeur and authority. A good example is Buland Darwaza in Fatehpur Sikri. It was added to the series of gateways in Akbar's walled fortress, to mark his victory over Gujarat.

Buland Darwaza, built in 1601

Minarets

A *minar* (minaret) is the place from where the call to prayer is sent out by a *muezzin* (announcer). Completed in 1220, the 240-ft (73-m) Qutub Minar was built to be a symbol of victory and faith—and to celebrate the power of the Delhi Sultanate.

Pietra dura from Taj Mahal, Agra

Nishat Bagh, Srinagar

Pietra dura

Emperor Jahangir imported from Florence the technique of pietra dura, or fitting slivers of precious and semiprecious stones into marble. The Taj Mahal is decorated with exquisite pietra dura, which was developed in Agra as *parchin kari*.

Water gardens

Water is an important part of an Islamic *charbagh*—a garden with four equal parts divided by water channels to recreate the Islamic Garden of Paradise. The *charbagh* at Nishat Bagh was built in 1633, for Asif Khan, Emperor Shah Jahan's father-in-law.

Qutub Complex, Delhi

Domes

A typical Persian architectural feature, the dome was introduced to India by the Delhi Sultanate. Its bulbous shape signifies heaven. With a huge, central dome, surrounded by smaller, blue domes, the tomb of Isa Khan reflects a blend of Imperial and Mughal styles.

Isa Khan's Tomb, Delhi

Arches

India saw its first true arches under the Delhi Sultanate. While the earlier arches were built by fitting together large blocks of stone, true arches were built with the help of a keystone in the center. The ornately carved Great Arch at the Qutub Complex is an early example.

Charminar

A well-known landmark in Hyderabad, the Charminar is named after its four tall minarets. It was built in 1591 during the reign of Muhammad Quli Qutb Shah. The four open archways on each side are in the Indo-Islamic style, while the stucco (plaster) floral motifs on the ceiling and walls are of Hindu influence.

Golconda Fort

The Qutb Shahi rulers (1518–1687) expanded the fort's original 12th-century mud structure into an enormous fortified city with palaces, mosques, and gardens.

Gol Gumbaz

The circular-domed tomb of Adil Shah, the ruler of Bijapur, was completed in 1656. It is famed for the "Whispering Gallery," where you can hear the faintest ticking of a watch!

Deccan Sultanate

The mid-16th to late 17th centuries saw the rise of the kingdoms of Bijapur, Golconda, Bidar, Berar, and Ahmednagar, known collectively as the Deccan Sultanate. The architecture of this period was a mix of Indo-Islamic and regional styles, with Persian and Central Asian elements.

Agra Fort

The Mughal royal residence was based in Agra in the 15th and 16th centuries. An imposing, red sandstone fort with courtly buildings was built here during Akbar's reign. These were expanded and embellished by Jahangir and Shah Jahan.

Fatehpur Sikri

Akbar laid the foundations of the "City of Victory" in 1569 to celebrate his victory over the Rajput kings. The legacy of Mughal architecture can be seen in its royal quarters, pavilions, gardens, and a public courtyard—Diwan-i-Am.

Anguri Bagh
Used by the Mughals for harvesting grapes and flowers, Anguri Bagh is made up of 85 symmetrical gardens.

Calligraphy
Inscriptions were carved in stone, such as the calligraphy seen on the tomb of Salim Chishti, Akbar's spiritual guide.

Mughal monuments

The Mughals (1526–1761) brought a large part of India together, establishing a rich culture that borrowed equally from Hindu and Muslim traditions. The Indo-Islamic architecture that thrived under their rule is admired the world over for its unique qualities of elegance and splendor—the Mughal style.

Itmad-ud-Daulah's Tomb

Designed like a mini Taj Mahal, this tomb, in Agra, was built in 1628 for the "Lord Treasurer" of the Mughal state. Its delicate style, favored by Shah Jahan, marks the transition from Akbar's sturdy red sandstone architecture to marble.

Red Fort

Commissioned by Shah Jahan, the Red Fort served as the royal residence from 1648 until 1856. The fort's main entrance, Lahore Gate, is where the Indian prime minister raises the flag every year on the Independence Day.

Chhatri
This roof-top feature was borrowed from Rajasthan.

Latticed screens
Jaalis are latticed screens, with intricate patterns carved out, allowing light and air into a building.

Carved relief
The red sandstone walls of the fort are decorated with delicately carved geometric and floral patterns.

! WOW!

Shah Jahan called the Red Fort Qila-i-Mubarak ("Auspicious Citadel").

The Great Mughal

Akbar was proclaimed emperor in 1556. With his military victories, he created a vast empire controlled by a centralized government. His secular approach to government helped to unify the realm, which he ruled until his death in 1605.

Akbar's tomb, Sikandara

Taj Mahal

Emperor Shah Jahan celebrated his love for his favorite queen Mumtaz Mahal in this jewel of Mughal architecture, in Agra. Designed as a mausoleum to contain her tomb, in 1632, the Taj Mahal is an example of symmetry and grace.

Making a masterpiece

It took 20,000 artisans 22 years to complete the Taj! The ultimate Mughal garden tomb, it was built to represent paradise on earth.

Minaret
Each minaret has a *chhatri*, or canopy, on top.

The creator
Poet-king Shah Jahan's rule (1627–1658) was marked by the nurturing of art and culture, as well as beautiful architecture.

The inspiration
Built for Shah Jahan's grandfather, Humayun's Tomb was the first garden tomb built in India and the inspiration behind the Taj's design.

Finial
The main dome's bronze finial (spire) was originally made of gold.

Dome
Although the dome has an onion-shaped exterior, the inner ceiling has straight sides.

! WOW!

The Taj is built in white marble, since white is the color of mourning in Islam.

Mosques

India's earliest mosques date back to the 7th century CE. Mosques grew in number following the start of Islamic rule in 1193. The styles may differ, but all mosques have domes, minarets, and a courtyard where worshippers pray facing the direction of Mecca—the site of Islam's most sacred shrine.

Bara Imambara

Lucknow's Bara Imambara was built as a large ceremonial hall, in 1784, to celebrate Muharram. The complex includes the Asafi Mosque, also known as Shahi Masjid, and the lavishly decorated Rumi Darwaza.

Makkah Masjid

This large mosque was completed in 1694, with bricks from Mecca that were used to build its central arch. Several rulers of Hyderabad are buried here.

Haji Ali

The shrine of a 15th-century Uzbek Sufi saint, Haji Ali Shah Bukhari, stands on a small island connected to the Mumbai shore by a long causeway. A dazzling white mosque was built here in the 20th century.

Moti Masjid

The pearly shine of its white marble gives Delhi's Moti Masjid its name. Built in 1659 as Aurangzeb's private mosque within the Red Fort, it has three rounded domes and a delicate, latticed screen through which the courtyard can be seen.

Jama Masjid

With soaring minarets flanking its three enormous domes, Delhi's Jama Masjid is one of the largest mosques in India. Its courtyard can hold 25,000 people. This masterpiece of Mughal architecture was completed in 1656.

Amber Fort

Like any typical fort, the forts in Rajasthan were citadels on hilltops, protecting the city below. Standing atop a natural ridge, Amber Fort was the seat of the Kachhwaha dynasty between the 11th and 18th centuries. The current structure, with gateways covered in mirrorwork, frescoes, and mosaics, was built in 1592 under Raja Man Singh.

Amber Fort, Amer

A ceremonial gateway for royal processions, Ganesh Pol lies at the heart of Amber Fort.

Rajasthani architecture

Ruled by several Rajput dynasties over centuries, Rajasthan evolved a distinct architecture, mixing local traditions and craftsmanship with the Mughal style.

Vijaya Stambha, Chittorgarh

Moosi Maharani ki Chhatri, Alwar

Chhatri
Chhatris are open pavilions with domes sitting on top of them. They are widely used in Rajasthani palaces and forts.

Sculptures
Fine carvings of gods and royalty are an important feature of Rajasthani architecture.

Patwon Ki Haveli, Jaisalmer

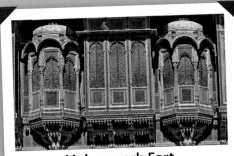

Mehrangarh Fort, Jodhpur

Jharokha
Jharokhas are balconies that were used to observe the proceedings in the courtyards below.

Haveli
A *haveli* s a luxurious mansion built for wealthy merchants and ministers. Most have a stone façade with fine carvings.

Suhaag Mandir, Amber Fort, Amer

Jaali
Stone screens allowed people to observe street life without being seen, while also letting in light and air.

Chand Baori, Jaipur

Baoli
Baolis or *baoris* are stepwells that were used to harvest water. During hot summers, the *baoli* provided relief to people who would gather there for cool air.

Forts and palaces of Rajasthan

Many spectacular forts and palaces, built under several Rajput kings, sprawl across the hills and lakes of Rajasthan. Some have been turned into hotels, while others remain preserved as monuments.

JAISALMER FORT

Located in: Jaisalmer
Built of yellow sandstone and unique to Jaisalmer's quarries, Jaisalmer Fort is also known as the Golden Fort. In 1156, King Rawal Jaisal commissioned the construction of the fort, in the heart of the Thar Desert.

Rajasthani paintings

Known for the use of bright colors and stylized figures, Rajasthani works have both religious and secular (nonreligious) themes. Miniatures on manuscripts or paintings on the walls of palaces and forts were common.

Mural of a royal procession, Mehrangarh Fort

JAL MAHAL

Located in: Jaipur
Built in the middle of Man Sagar Lake, Jal Mahal was built in the 18th century for duck-hunting parties held by King Madho Singh I. The water palace was inspired by a similar palace in Udaipur where the king spent his childhood.

CHITTOR FORT

Located in: Chittorgarh
Founded in 728 CE, Chittor served as the capital of Mewar. A key event in the fort's history was the Siege of Chittorgarh. Alauddin Khalji, a ruler from the Delhi Sultanate, conquered Chittor after an eight-month-long seige.

MEHRANGARH FORT

Located in: Jodphur
Founded by Rao Jodha in 1459 CE, Mehrangarh Fort was developed further between the mid-17th and mid-19th centuries. Several palaces are found within the fort, protected by its high walls.

UMAID BHAWAN PALACE

Located in: Jodhpur
Commissioned by Maharaja Umaid Singh in 1929, the palace is built of sandstone and marble, with influences from Rajput, Jain, and European architectural styles. It is said that it took 3,000 men 15 years to complete it.

CITY PALACE

Located in: Udaipur
The largest palace in Rajasthan, City Palace was built over a period of 400 years under the Mewar dynasty. The architecture of the many palaces in the complex is a combination of both Rajput and Mughal styles.

Gwalior Fort

Mughal emperor Babar once described the Gwalior Fort as "the pearl among fortresses in India." With soaring towers and jagged battlements on a hill in the center of Gwalior city, the fort is said to be invincible.

Man Singh Palace

One of the many palaces in Gwalior Fort, it was commissioned in 1486 by Man Singh Tomar, a great patron of music. The palace has finely carved doorways and colorful mosaics, as well as latticed stone screens, behind which royal family members could learn music.

Motifs

Ornamental glazed tiles with unusual patterns in blue and yellow decorate the ramparts and the walls of the palaces housed within.

Seat of the Scindias
Ruled by a series of Hindu dynasties, Delhi Sultanate, and the Mughals, the fort was taken over by the Maratha Scindias in the 18th century.

In Man Singh's Palace

Mythical beasts carved out of stone support the sloped cornices (spaces where the roof meets the wall). These beasts, with the body of a lion and head of a boar, parrot, or elephant, are known as *shardulas*.

Jain tirthankaras

Sculptures of Jain *tirthankaras* were carved into the cliff face during the 15th century. These are sheltered within caves and niches close to the Gwalior Fort.

REALLY?

Within the fort is the tomb of Tansen, Akbar's famous court musician.

Golden Temple

The heart of Sikhism, the Golden Temple (Sri Harmandir Sahib), in Amritsar, is the chief *gurdwara* of the Sikhs. The original structure was rebuilt in the early 19th century, in marble and gold, under Ranjit Singh, who founded the mighty Sikh Empire in 1801.

Golden dome
Added in 1830, the gold foil on the domes gave the temple its name.

Everyday rituals

Guru Granth Sahib, the sacred Sikh scripture, is revered as a living entity and forms the core of worship in all *gurdwaras*. At the Golden Temple, the daily rituals revolve around Adi Granth Sahib, the first copy of Guru Granth Sahib, compiled in 1604 by Arjan Singh, the fifth Sikh guru.

Daily routine
The day begins with *prakash*, when the Adi Granth is taken out of bed and read aloud. At night, it is tucked in bed, in the closing ritual called *sukhasan*.

Clock tower
Once a clock tower built by the British, this building now serves as an entrance.

! **REALLY?**

A Sufi saint, Mian Mir, laid the foundation stone of the Golden Temple in the 16th century.

Amrit Sarovar
A man-made square pool, called *Amrit Sarovar* (Pool of Nectar), surrounds the temple.

Langar
A vital feature at the Golden Temple is *langar*, the community kitchen where meals are cooked and served to the worshippers.

Akal Takht
The highest seat of the Sikh authority, the Akal Takht is based in the Golden Temple. Hargobind, the sixth guru, set up Akal Takht in the 17th century. Today it plays a key role in upholding the values and heritage of the Sikh community.

Akal Takht, Golden Temple

Colonial monuments

Europeans first arrived in India as merchants. In the 17th century, they formed companies, building fortifications to defend their trading centers. As they started gaining territorial control, several buildings were created—known today as colonial monuments.

French

The French East India Company set up base in Pondicherry in 1673. The tiny fishing hamlet soon bloomed into a port town. Ruled by the French until 1954, Pondicherry still retains its colonial heritage, seen in the classical buildings in the French Quarter.

Our Lady of Angels Church, Pondicherry

Portuguese

The Portuguese ruled their territories, which included Goa, Daman, and Diu, until 1961. Their base for more than 450 years, Goa still bears a strong Portuguese influence, visible in its colonial-era buildings and Catholic churches.

Fort Diu, Daman and Diu

Gateway of India

Mumbai's iconic arch monument overlooks the Arabian Sea. The Gateway of India was created in 1911 to commemorate the visit of King George V. Scottish architect George Wittet took elements from Indo-Islamic and Gujarati styles to design this classical Roman triumphal arch. In its time, it stood as an imposing symbol of the British Empire in India.

Gateway of India, Mumbai

British

The British colonial era lasted from the early 1600s to 1947, leaving the most enduring impact on India's architecture. Starting with classical European, the British began to borrow from the local styles, creating impressive landmarks across India.

Viceregal Lodge, Shimla

Churches

The European colonizers brought missionaries to spread Christianity in India. They founded churches, basilicas, and cathedrals. Many of them still exist—from the vibrant Portuguese basilicas in Goa and the ornate churches in French Pondicherry to the British Indo-Saracenic gems.

Santa Cruz Basilica, Kochi

Some of India's earliest European churches were founded in the port city of Kochi. The Portuguese built this early 16th-century basilica in the Gothic style.

Basilica of Bom Jesus, Goa

This grand basilica was founded by the Jesuits in 1584. It contains a decorated silver casket holding the bodily remains of St. Francis Xavier, one of the first Jesuit priests.

St. Paul's Cathedral, Kolkata

The first cathedral to be built in a British colony, St. Paul's was earlier a church. Queen Victoria sent a gift of gilded silver plates to mark its consecration ceremony in 1847.

Immaculate Conception Cathedral, Pondicherry

The French Emperor Louis XIV funded the original late 17th-century church, which was rebuilt a century later as this cathedral.

All Saints' Cathedral, Allahabad

The British gained control of Allahabad in 1801, founding law courts, churches, and the university. Designed by William Emerson, this Gothic cathedral was built in 1877.

St. Mary's Basilica, Bengaluru

This basilica traces its origins to a modest, 17th-century thatched shrine built by local Christians. A French architect designed its current structure in the 19th century.

Indo-Saracenic architecture

A vibrant mix of European and Indian styles, the Indo-Saracenic style was developed in the late 19th century to represent the power of the British Empire. It was used mostly by British architects to design public buildings, and private palaces for the rajahs (princes).

English Gothic
The tower was initially intended as a clock tower, but the plan was abandoned. Elements from English Gothic churches along with Mughal *chhatris* were used in its design.

Mughal
Mughal-style arches, seen on the exterior, form windows with *jaalis* (latticed screens), and *chhatris* (protruding eaves), which the Mughals borrowed from Rajasthan.

Venetian
The Venetian domes are topped by ribbed lanterns, which are borrowed from Islamic architecture.

Laxmi Vilas Palace, Vadodara
The princely states loyal to the British Raj built lavish residential palaces. Maharaja Sayajirao III, a Gaekwad ruler, commissioned Charles Mant to design this Indo-Saracenic palace, which was completed in 1890.

The British Raj

India was brought under the British Empire in 1858, with Queen Victoria crowned as the Empress of India. The princely states were left in the care of rajahs, who remained loyal to the Crown. The era, known as the British Raj, lasted until India's freedom in 1947. The public buildings created during the Raj, especially in the colonial cities of Bombay, Delhi, Calcutta, and Madras, left a deep imprint on India's architecture.

Madras High Court, established in 1862

Medal struck to celebrate Queen Victoria's Golden Jubilee in 1887

Rajasthani

This area was the *zenana*, quarters reserved only for women. Elements from Rajasthani architecture, such as the *shikharas* from Hindu temples as well as floral motifs and vines, can be seen here.

Maratha

The lotus dome on top of the central area, reserved only for the Maharaja, bears a strong Maratha influence.

Mysore Palace

The Wodeyars, who continued to rule Mysore under the British rule, commissioned architect Henry Irwin to design this lavish Indo-Saracenic palace in 1898. Decorated with exquisite carvings and artifacts, the Mysore Palace houses a priceless collection of artworks from around the world.

Regal splendor

The palace still serves as the official residence of the Wodeyar dynasty, founded in 1399. The Wodeyars are one of the wealthiest former royal families in India.

Durbar Hall
The Wodeyars once held meetings in the magnificent gold-and-turquoise hall. Goddess Durga in her many forms is depicted in a series of paintings on the rear wall.

Kalyana Mantapa
The marriage pavilion, or Kalyana Mantapa, was built for hosting royal weddings. The glazed tiles used in its flooring were imported from England.

Royal Dasara
Devotees of Goddess Durga, the Wodeyars celebrate Dussehra, or Dasara, every year at the palace for 10 days.

The demon Mahishasura, who was defeated and killed by Goddess Durga

Victoria Memorial

Lord Curzon was the Viceroy of India from 1899 to 1905. He commissioned Kolkata's iconic monument in memory of Queen Victoria, whose statue stands at the entrance. The grounds of this Indo-Saracenic masterpiece include 25 galleries, which feature British Raj memorabilia.

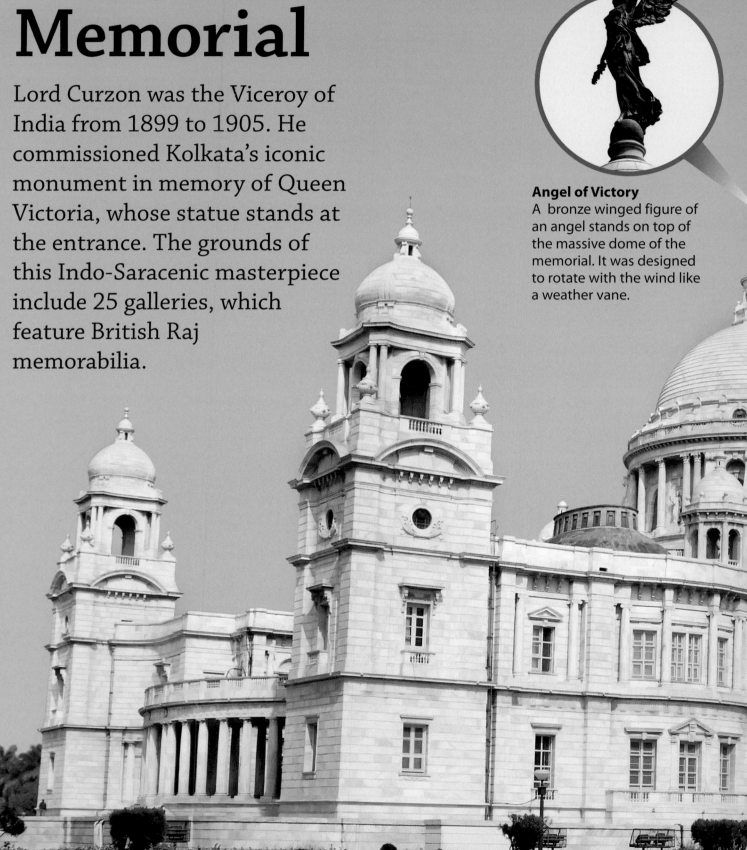

Angel of Victory
A bronze winged figure of an angel stands on top of the massive dome of the memorial. It was designed to rotate with the wind like a weather vane.

Victoria Terminus (VT)

With tall spires, arches, and domes, VT is an impressive example of Victorian Gothic architecture in India. It was built to celebrate Queen Victoria's Golden Jubilee, and is still one of the busiest train stations in Mumbai.

Victoria Terminus, now known as Chhatrapati Shivaji Terminus

Bronze panel
Sir Goscombe John created this bronze panel of the viceroy's procession to decorate the pedestal below Queen Victoria's statue. Warriors, musicians, children, and animals are shown as part of the procession.

! WOW!

Victoria Memorial is made of the same marble as Taj Mahal!

Statue of Lord Curzon

Rashtrapati Bhavan

Edwin Lutyens designed this imposing structure in 1912. It was meant to be the crowning glory of Delhi, which had been named the capital of British India in 1911. A symbol of power since it first served as the residence of the British Viceroy, the Rashtrapati Bhavan became the official home of the President of the democratic republic of India in 1950.

Independence

India won independence from the British rule in 1947. It became a democratic republic on January 26, 1950, the day its Constitution came into effect. Delhi, the former British imperial capital and a city that had played a crucial role in India's history, was made the capital of the new nation.

Parliament House

Sansad Bhavan
The Constitution of India was drafted in Parliament House. Built in 1927 for the lower house of imperial legislature during the British Raj, today, it hosts all parliamentary sessions.

The monumental Jaipur column was sponsored by Maharaja Madho Singh of Jaipur.

Nehru being sworn in as the first Prime Minister by President Rajendra Prasad

Central Secretariat

Formation of the government
The newly formed government was led by Rajendra Prasad and Jawaharlal Nehru. A key figure in Indian politics until his death in 1964, Nehru commissioned many new monuments.

Administration of the country
India's seat of power, the Central Secretariat houses the key ministries and the Prime Minister's Office (PMO). Dholpur sandstone from Rajasthan was used to build this Herbert Baker-designed structure.

Modern monuments

A major part of nation-building was breaking free from the past and creating India's modern identity. The monuments built after 1947 reflect a desire to create something new, while borrowing from the local architectural styles, as well as the colonial legacy. Yet, many buildings were designed in the individual styles of architects and city planners, changing much of India's landscape for good.

Le Corbusier's Chandigarh

Nehru appointed Swiss-French Le Corbusier to turn Chandigarh into a new city, "unfettered by the past." Of the many marvels Le Corbusier created, the Assembly (1962) reflects his signature style in its open spaces.

IIM Ahmedabad

In 1961, American architect Louis Kahn joined BV Doshi to design this exposed-brick building, using local brick and concrete. Geometric shapes were carved out of the exterior to allow light and air into spaces fit for modern teaching methods.

Vidhana Soudha

The seat of state legislature in Bangalore, Vidhana Soudha was built in 1956—the year Karnataka was formed, transferring power from the Wodeyars. Designed by BR Manickam, its post-independence Neo-Dravidian architecture is a modern expression of the Dravidian style.

Baha'i Lotus Temple

Designed by Fariborz Sahba to resemble the Sydney Opera House, this intriguing marble structure has no straight lines, but 27 "petals" forming the lotus shape. It was built in 1986 as a prayer hall for the members of the Baha'i community.

! WOW!
The apex of the Baha'i Temple is open, reflecting light into the central prayer hall.

Meet an expert

Inspired by his history teacher and love for all things old, Ratish Nanda became a conservation architect. He has been working for the Aga Khan Trust for Culture (AKTC) since 1999 and helped conserve more than 100 monuments in Delhi alone.

Q: What does a conservation architect do?

A: Conservation architects are trained to take care of our historic buildings, much like doctors take care of us. Heritage structures need experts who understand traditional materials and building techniques.

Q: Why did you want to be a conservation architect?

A: As a kid I was fascinated with the 16th-century domed monuments of Delhi. Once I completed my architecture studies, I did a postgraduation in historic building conservation.

Q: What's the most exciting part of your job?

A: To be able to contribute toward giving a new lease on life to a ruin. To restore the grandeur as designed by the medieval architects is very satisfying and exciting.

Q: Which project do you cherish the most?

A: For the AKTC, I helped restore a 16th-century garden in Kabul, Afghanistan. Here, conservation works were meant to provide a healing touch to a bruised city and its people. To have helped convert the ruins of Bagh-e Babur from a dust bowl to a lush green garden with flowing water, now drawing 40,000 visitors every week, was the most meaningful work I ever did.

Q: What memories do you have of Delhi's monuments?

A: We are lucky in Delhi to have more than 1,000 years of continuous history, although only a few hundred historic buildings survive today. For me, living and working among these buildings from another age defines Delhi.

Craftsmen installing gold finial atop Humayun's Tomb

Q: What drew you toward the conservation of Humayun's Tomb?

A: I have always felt blessed to have been able to lead the AKTC team to get Humayun's Tomb back into the pink of health. It's a great monument, precursor to the Taj Mahal, and deserved all the care it needed. Over 500,000 man-days of work by master craftsmen were required to conserve Humayun's Tomb, which helped create a lot of jobs.

Humayun's Tomb after restoration

Q: Which historical gardens have you restored?

A: In 1997, on the 50th anniversary of India's Independence, the Aga Khan gifted the garden restoration of Humayun's Tomb to India. Since then we have restored the Bagh-e Babur in Kabul, Isa Khan's garden tomb and, more recently, the wonderful Sunder Nursery in Delhi. In all these garden restorations, landscape architect M Shaheer was a key partner.

Q: Is landscape restoration as satisfying as conserving heritage buildings?

A: Ideally, monuments should be kept in their original setting, which is rarely possible due to modern buildings. Thus, it is immensely satisfying to restore gardens within which monuments once stood. This also creates a space for people to enjoy nature. Six monuments in Sunder Nursery have since been added to UNESCO's World Heritage list—the highest honor I could have hoped for.

Q: What is a typical day like for a conservation architect?

A: A conservation architect's life revolves around the phases that a monument requires for its conservation. These include documentation of the problem, archival research to understand a monument's past, identifying the work that will help ensure it is passed on to future generations in a better state than we inherited it in, and, finally, close supervision of repair work. Government approvals and public support are equally important, too.

Q: What advice do you have for future conservationists?

A: A career in conservation is for architects, historians, scientists, and archaeologists, among others. It is meaningful and gives life a sense of achievement and purpose. Working with the government, however, requires a lot of determination and patience.

Facts and figures

There are many Indian monuments, and even though some of them are thousands of years old, they are still amazing. Read on to learn facts and figures about some of these monuments.

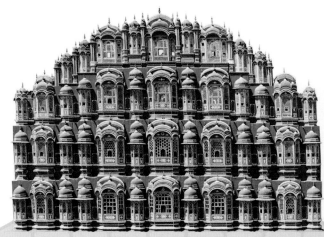

HAWA MAHAL IN JAIPUR, RAJASTHAN, HAS A HONEYCOMB-LIKE EXTERIOR, WHICH IS MADE UP OF 953 WINDOWS.

The Cellular Jail, a former British jail on the Andaman Islands, held around 80,000 political prisoners during India's freedom movement.

Model of the Cellular Jail

The Howrah Bridge in Kolkata was built without a single nut and bolt, but with **rivets**.

23.6 MILES

is the length of the walls of Kumbhalgarh Fort in Rajasthan. This makes it one of the longest fortified walls in the world!

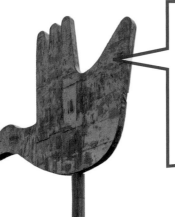

The Open Hand Monument, architect Le Corbusier's dream project, was built in Chandigarh, 20 years after his death.

Built in the shape of a ship on a small island near Diu, Pani Kotha, or Fortim-do-Mar, was once a Portuguese prison complex.

Mysore Palace, built in the early 20th century, cost about **41 lakh**. That is around **211 crore** rupees today!

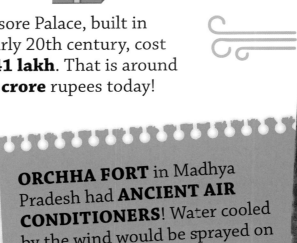

ORCHHA FORT in Madhya Pradesh had **ANCIENT AIR CONDITIONERS**! Water cooled by the wind would be sprayed on the roof of the palace to cool it.

3 months

is the amount of time that the Turkish invaders took, in the 13th century, to burn down the vast collection of texts housed in the library of Nalanda University in Bihar.

13,300

names of Indian soldiers of the British Indian army, who died in World War I, are inscribed on the surface of India Gate, Delhi.

Glossary

Here are the meanings of some words that are useful for you to know when learning all about the monuments of India.

Bodhisattva In Buddhism, one who is capable of attaining freedom from the cycle of birth-death-rebirth (nirvana), but delays it in order to help others in attaining it.

calligraphy Art of creating beautiful, stylized handwriting by using a special pen or brush

cantilever bridge Type of bridge that is built using structures supported only at one end

chhajja Projecting or overhanging cover of a roof, largely used in Rajasthani architecture

chaitya Buddhist prayer hall for monks to gather and worship together; contains a stupa at one end (usually without a relic that a typical stupa houses)

charbagh Persian-style garden which is divided into four equal parts by water

channels, based on the Islamic idea of four rivers flowing in the "garden of paradise;" a distinctive feature of Mughal architecture, especially the Taj Mahal

chhattri Literally meaning an "umbrella;" a raised, dome-shaped canopy, used in Indian architecture

citadel Stronghold or fortified building on high ground in or near a city

enlightenment In Buddhism, the state in which one is free from the cycle of rebirth; also known as nirvana

finial Decorative element added above the spire of a building

fresco Type of wall painting in which paint is applied when the plaster is still wet

garden tomb A tomb or mausoleum with a beautiful garden surrounding it

gopuram Heavily decorated, pyramid-shaped gate, which forms the entrance of a typical Hindu temple in southern India

Gothic Style of architecture that developed in Europe from the 12th to the 16th century, used mostly in building cathedrals and churches; its main features are tall pillars, pointed arches, and curved ceilings

jaali Perforated stone, or latticed screen, usually with geometric patterns, found in medieval Indian architecture

Jain A person who follows Jainism, an ancient Indian religion

Jesuits Members of one of the Roman Catholic orders

jharokha Rajasthani-style enclosed balcony, jutting out of the wall

Maitreya Bodhisattva and "Future Buddha," who will be born as the next human Buddha

Mamluks Former slaves of Muhammad of Ghur (modern-day Afghanistan), one of whom—Qutbuddin Aibak—gained control of his territories in India, establishing the Delhi Sultanate in 1206

mausoleum Building containing a tomb or a group of tombs

minar Tower, or minaret

miniature paintings Small detailed painting

mosaic Picture or pattern created by using small pieces of materials such as stone or glass

motif Recurring design, or pattern, used in art

mural Wall painting in which paint is applied on dry plaster

parchin kari Mughal-style inlay work derived from pietra dura; reached its peak during the reign of Shah Jahan

prakash Also called "parkash," it refers to the morning ritual held at a gurdwara, when the holy book of the Sikhs, the Granth Sahib, is carried to the prayer hall and opened by the head priest

petroglyph Drawing or carving on rock, especially a prehistoric one

pietra dura Decorative art involving the use of shaped and polished pieces of colorful stones to create patterns

prehistory Period before recorded history

ratha Literally meaning "chariot," the word is used for a Hindu shrine shaped like a chariot, such as the chariot-shaped temples of Konark and Mamallapuram

relief Carving or sculpture on a flat surface

scripture Holy book or sacred writings of any religion

shikhara Tower, or spire, of a typical Nagara-style temple

Sufi Muslim ascetic who believes in experiencing God directly through love and devotion, rather than by performing rituals and reading scriptures

stucco Plaster of any kind that is used for coating walls; also used as molded shapes and figures to decorate the exterior of a building

stupa Mound-shaped structure typically containing the remains of the Buddha or a Buddhist monk or nun

sukhasana Evening ritual performed at a gurdwara, when the Guru Granth Sahib (the holy book of the Sikhs) is closed

Tirthankara Past births of Lord Mahavira; the word literally means the founder of "tirth," or the passage across the sea of births and deaths, leading to nirvana

torana Free-standing gateway, usually decorative, used in Buddhist, Jain, and Hindu architecture

triumphal arch Arch built to celebrate a victory, or to honor an important event or person

true arch Arch built with the help of a central stone or keystone

vihara Buddhist monastery, with accommodation for monks and nuns; a shrine with an image of the Buddha, and space for prayer and meditation

vimana Pyramid-shaped structure built above the main shrine of a typical Dravidian-style temple

Index

Acknowledgements

The publishers would like to thank: Andrew Korah and Shambhavi Thatte for editorial assistance; Radhika Haswani for proofreading; Kartik Gera and Jaileen Kaur for design support; Ranjana Sengupta for historical consultation; Shannon Beatty for Americanization; and Malavika Talukder for her valuable insight.

The publisher would like to thank the following for their kind permission to reproduce their photographs:

(Key: a-above; b-below/bottom; c-center; f-far; l-left; r-right; t-top)

1 Dreamstime.com: Byelikova. **2 Dreamstime.com**: Dmitry Rukhlenko (crb). **3 Dreamstime.com**: Phuongphoto (crb/Bronze panel); Thitisaichua (crb); Toby Williams (b). **4–5 Dreamstime.com**: Marina Pissarova. **5 Dreamstime.com**: Kampee Patisena (cr); Pzaxe (cra); Marina Pissarova (crb). **6 Dreamstime.com**: Arindam Banerjee (bl); Samrat35 (cr); Mcmorabad (br). **7 Dreamstime.com**: Dr. pramod Bansode (tl); Mdsindia (cr); Mohamed Abdul Rasheed (clb); EPhotocorp (br). **8–9 Dreamstime.com**: Leslie Clary. **10–11 Dreamstime.com**: Saiko3p. **10 Dreamstime.com**: Henning Marquardt (cb). **11 Dreamstime.com**: Tinnaporn Sathapornnanont (c); Toby Williams (ca). **12 Dreamstime.com**: Aapthamithra (br). **13 Dreamstime.com**: Aliaksandr Mazurkevich (bc). **14–15 Dreamstime.com**: Sanga Park. **14 Dreamstime.com**: Shailendra Sood (bc). **15 Dreamstime.com**: Saiko3p (ca, cr, bc). **16 Dreamstime.com**: Steve Allen (c); Dmitry Rukhlenko (cra). **17 Dreamstime.com**: Elilarionova (cl); EPhotocorp (tr, cr). **18 Dreamstime.com**: Steve Allen (bc); Jeewee (cl). **18–19 Dreamstime.com**: Dmitry Rukhlenko (bc). **19 Dreamstime.com**: Henning Marquardt (cb). **20–21 Dreamstime.com**: Rafał Cichawa (c). **21 Dreamstime.com**: Beat Germann (clb); Saiko3p (cr). **24 Dreamstime.com**: Mario Savoia (bl). **25 Dreamstime.com**: Antonella865 (br); Pratik Panda (tr). **26–27 Dreamstime.com**: Ujjaldey (c). **27 Dreamstime.com**: Stuart Atkinson (cr); Gaurav Masand (cra). **28 Dreamstime.com**: Iuliia Kryzhevska (clb); Takepicsforfun (cl); Pascalou95 (cr); Zatletic (crb). **29 Dreamstime.com**: Faurem (br); Szefei (cr); Juritt62 (clb). **30–31 Dreamstime.com**: Elenatur (c). 30 Narendra Swain, Aga Khan

Trust for Culture: (bl). The Metropolitan Museum of Art: Rogers Fund and The Kevorkian Foundation Gift (cl). **32 Dreamstime.com**: Leonid Andronov (bc); Saiko3p (tl); Steve Estvanik (tr). **32–33 Dreamstime.com**: Ovydyborets (Background). **33 Dreamstime.com**: Saiko3p (r). **34–35 Dreamstime.com**: Rafał Cichawa (t). **35 Dreamstime.com**: Nilanjan Bhattacharya (cr); Prasert Meeintha (tr); Attila Jandi (ca); Rene Drouyer (c); Kattiya Loukobkul (crb). **36 Dreamstime.com**: Donyanedomam (cra); Jeremy Richards (bl); Dreamstation (crb). **37 Dreamstime.com**: Daniel Boiteau (clb); Christophe Cappelli (cla); Yurataranik (cra); Saiko3p (crb). **38 Dreamstime.com**: Dmitry Rukhlenko (cl, bc). **38–39 Dreamstime.com**: Dmitry Rukhlenko (c). **39 Dreamstime.com**: Steve Allen (cr); Mcmorabad (tc). **40 Dorling Kindersley**: Christopher Pillitz (br). **40–41 Dreamstime.com**: Dmitry Rukhlenko (c). **41 Dorling Kindersley**: Christopher Pillitz (bl). **Dreamstime.com**: Steve Allen (br). **42 Alamy Stock Photo**: Shailendra Sood (br). **Dreamstime.com**: Stuart Atkinson (bl). **43 Dreamstime.com**. **44 Dreamstime.com**: Dr Ajay Kumar Singh (crb); Denis Vostrikov (clb); Saiko3p (tr). **45 Dreamstime.com**: Stuart Atkinson (clb); Suronin (tl); Klodien (r). **46–47 Dreamstime.com**: Povarov (Background). **Getty Images**: India Picture / UIG (b). **47 Dreamstime.com**: Dharshani Gk Arts (tl). The Metropolitan Museum of Art: Gift of Assunta Sommella Peluso, Ada Peluso, and Romano I. Peluso, in memory of Ignazio Peluso, 2001 (ca). **48 Dreamstime.com**: Christian Ouellet (bc). **48–49 Dreamstime.com**: Amith Nag (bc); Noppasin Wongchum (c). **49 Dreamstime.com**: Prashant Vaidya (cb); Denis Vostrikov (bc). **50 Dreamstime.com**: Zatletic (cra). **50–51 Dreamstime.com**: Oleg Doroshenko (b). **51 Dreamstime.com**: Phuongphoto (c); Thitisaichua (c/Photo frame); Saiko3p (tr). **52–53 Dreamstime.com**: Saiko3p (c). **52 Dreamstime.com**: Iryna Rasko (crb). **53 Photo Division, PIB, Ministry of Information and Broadcasting**: (clb). **54 Dreamstime.com**: Ghanshyam P

Ramchandani (br); Saiko3p (cl). **55 Dreamstime.com**: Ajay Bhaskar (tr); Saiko3p (c). **56 Narendra Swain, Aga Khan Trust for Culture**: (tr, br). **57 Narendra Swain, Aga Khan Trust for Culture**: (tr). **58 Dreamstime.com**: Byelikova (tr); Subhrajyoti Parida (cr); Sharad Raval (b). **58–59 Dreamstime.com**: William Bode (bc). **59 Dreamstime.com**: Steve Allen (bc); Saiko3p (cla); Anandoart (tr); Mcmorabad (cr). **60 Dreamstime.com**: Henning Marquardt (tl). **64 Dreamstime.com**: Aliaksandr Mazurkevich (tr).

Endpaper images: *Front*: **Dreamstime.com**: Photo 82536423 © Dr Ajay Kumar Singh - Dreamstime.com crb, Dr Ajay Kumar Singh bc, Inderkant tl, Gaurav Masand br, Mdsindia ca, Yogesh Raut cra, Shariqkhan tc, Maneesh Upadhyay cl, Zastavkin cr; *Back*: **Dorling Kindersley:** The University of Aberdeen tl; **Dreamstime.com**: EPhotocorp cr, Pablo Hidalgo tr, Jayv bc (Red Fort), Suronin bc; **Library of Congress, Washington, D.C.**: George Grantham Bain Collection ca; **Photo Division, PIB, Ministry of Information and Broadcasting**: br; **The Metropolitan Museum of Art**: Rogers Fund and The Kevorkian Foundation Gift bl.

Cover images: *Front*: **Alamy Stock Photo**: Joana Kruse bl; **Dorling Kindersley**: National Museum, New Delhi c; **Dreamstime.com**: Aliaksandr Mazurkevich br; **Narendra Swain, Aga Khan Trust for Culture**: cra; *Back*: **Dreamstime.com**: Henning Marquardt clb, Saiko3p cla, crb; *Spine*: **Dreamstime.com**: Henning Marquardt b.

All other images © Dorling Kindersley
For further information see:
www.dkimages.com

My Findout facts:

Timeline of monuments

Akbar moves the Mughal capital to Fatehpur Sikri.

Jantar Mantar, commissioned by Sawai Jai Singh II, is completed in Jaipur. It is the largest of the five astronomical observatories built during his reign.

Coins issued by the East India Company

British East India Company is formed and gets trading rights with India, establishing its first factory in Machilipatnam.

Bahadur Shah Zafar II

The last Mughal is exiled. British East India Company is disbanded and British Raj begins in India.

1572	1600–1615	1632–1656	1661	1734	1799	1858

← Continued from front of book

Bombay, a Portuguese territory, is given as a dowry of the Portuguese princess on her marriage to the English king, Charles II.

Mysore kingdom fights wars against the British, which results in British victory and the death of Tipu Sultan. British allies, Wodeyars are installed as rulers.

Gumbaz at Srirangapatnam, housing Tipu Sultan's grave

Shah Jahan commissions several monuments, most significantly, Red Fort, Taj Mahal, and Jama Masjid.